FAT PI

Neil LaBute

BROADWAY PLAY PUBLISHING INC
224 E 62nd St, NY, NY 10065
www.broadwayplaypub.com
info@broadwayplaypub.com

First printing: March 2014
I S B N: 978-0-88145-520-5

Book design: Marie Donovan
Page make-up: Adobe Indesign
Typeface: Palatino
Printed and bound in the U S A

FAT PIG had its world premiere at Manhattan Class Company Theater in New York.

"That first meeting with her"

(*A woman [*HELEN*] in a crowded restaurant. Standing at one of those tall tables. A bunch of food in front of her and she is quietly eating it. By the way, she's a plus size. Very*)

(*After a moment, a man [*TOM*] enters juggling a lunch tray. He glances around, then moves toward her.*)

TOM: …Pretty big.

HELEN: Excuse me?

TOM: I'm sorry, I was just sort of, you know, speaking out loud. Pretty big in here. That's what I was saying…

HELEN: Oh. Right.

TOM: Lot of room for, you know, people.

HELEN: Yes. It's popular.

(TOM *looks around, trying to see if there's a spot for him yet.*)

TOM: And yet nowhere to…actually…

HELEN: You can eat here if you want.

TOM: No, I don't need to, umm…

HELEN: What?

TOM: I dunno, I hadn't really thought the rest of that one through! Ahh, "intrude", I guess.

HELEN: You're not. I'll make some room for you.

TOM: You sure?

HELEN: Of course.

TOM: Thanks.

(HELEN *slides some of her food to one side, allowing* TOM *a space if he wants it. He takes the spot. Silence*)

HELEN: ...I thought you meant me. Before.

TOM: I'm sorry?

HELEN: When you said that, "pretty big", I thought you were saying that to me. About me.

TOM: Oh, no, God no! I wouldn't...you did?

HELEN: For a second.

TOM: No, that'd be...you know. Rude.

HELEN: Still...

TOM: I mean, why would I do that? A thing like that? I'm not...

HELEN: You'd be surprised. People say all kinds of things here.

TOM: In this place?

HELEN: No, not just here, this restaurant or anything, I mean in the city.

TOM: So...you mean, people actually...what? Say things to your face?

HELEN: Of course. All the time.

TOM: About what?

(HELEN *looks over at* TOM *without saying anything. Silence*)

HELEN: ...my hair color. *(Beat)* What do you think?

TOM: Oh, I see. *(Smiles)*

HELEN: It's not a huge deal—I was just mentioning it.

TOM: Yeah, but...

HELEN: You get used to it. I guess they think that, I don't know, after a certain size or whatever...

TOM: Geez, that's hard to...

HELEN: ...I shouldn't have all this stuff for lunch, anyway, but...I'm hungry.

TOM: Sure...hey, it's lunchtime, right?

HELEN: Yeah.

TOM: I mean, look at me...look how much chicken they put on my salad!

HELEN: That's not exactly comforting...

TOM: I just meant...whatever. Sorry.

HELEN: I had three pieces of pizza, the garlic bread, and a salad. Plus dessert...

TOM: Hey, you know...it's your...

HELEN: How does that sentence end?

TOM: Badly, I'm sure! Hell, it's your body, you do what you want. That's what I think...

HELEN: Really?

TOM: Of course. I mean...

HELEN: So, do you really like sprouts or does that only hold true for me? Your little theory there...

TOM: No, I'm just...I had a really big breakfast, so I'm...

HELEN: That's a lie.

TOM: Ahh, yeah. Yes, it was. You saw through that one...damn, you seem pretty good at this!

HELEN: What, the truth?

TOM: Yeah, that.

HELEN: I'm not bad, actually...not too bad at all.

(*A moment between* HELEN *and* TOM, *then they both get down to some serious eating.*)

HELEN: You work nearby?

TOM: No...I'm just up here for this meeting. Usually I eat downtown. (*Beat*) And you?

HELEN: Yes, I'm over at the library. I was at an interview, actually, for a different branch...that's why I have the, you know, "Miss Kitty" hair today. All dolled up.

(TOM *nods and points at a plastic bag on the table.*)

TOM: Ahh, cool...I get it. Gunsmoke. You look nice. (*Grins*) Yeah, I saw the library bag earlier. Wow. (*Points*) That's a lot of videos there.

HELEN: ...it was a long weekend...

TOM: Right. (*Smiles*) So, lemme guess... *When Harry Met Sally*, *Sleepless in Seattle*, probably, ummm...The Notebook...

HELEN: Wrong! Take a look.

(HELEN *smiles at* TOM *as he reaches over and glances in the bag. Pulls a few out. Library emblem on each case.*)

TOM: *The Guns of Navarone, Where Eagles Dare...Ice Station Zebra*?

HELEN: I threw myself a little Alistair MacLean festival.

TOM: Huh. Don't get me wrong because I love that stuff, but...that's not very "girlie" of you.

HELEN: ...You're probably just dating the wrong kinds of girls.

(HELEN *and* TOM *share a grin and a chuckle. He reappraises her.*)

TOM: No doubt about that—I can't even call 'em "girls" without getting hit by a lawsuit, so... (*Smiles*) ...you're a librarian?

HELEN: Yeah. Well, we don't really use that term any more, but, ahh...

TOM: Sure, of course! It's probably, like,'printed word specialist' or something now, I suppose…

HELEN: Exactly. *(Beat)* They're always coming up with new names for stuff, something to make that person feel better…a "refuse technician" or what-have-you.

TOM: That's so true…

HELEN: Right? Problem is, you still find yourself picking shit up off the street, no matter what they call you! I mean…you know…

(TOM laughs at this and HELEN joins in. She makes a lovely sound as she goes at it. He studies her.)

TOM: …you have a terrific laugh.

HELEN: Thanks.

TOM: You're welcome. A potty mouth, but a really cute laugh…

HELEN: That's sweet, thank you! *(Laughs)* …Now that I'm so self-conscious that I'll never do it again.

TOM: Exactly!

(HELEN and TOM laugh together again and then don't know what to say next. They decide to take a bite of their meals instead.)

HELEN: How's that spinach coming along?

TOM: Mmmmmmmm…so darn good!

HELEN: Looks great.

TOM: Yeah. Yummy.

HELEN: The pizza's terrific here. I come by all the time for it…

TOM: I'll bet. *(Looks over at her)* I just mean…you know. If it's so good, I would understand. That. *(Beat)* Please-help-me…

HELEN: I get what you meant.

TOM: Great.

HELEN: You shouldn't be so nervous...I mean, if we're gonna start dating.

TOM: What?

HELEN: It's a joke.

TOM: Oh, right. Got it. Little slow!

(HELEN *and* TOM *laugh together. He looks around, self-consciously.*)

HELEN: I'm sorry. You should've seen your face...

TOM: What? No...

HELEN: I thought you were gonna choke on your avocado there...

TOM: That's not true, come on...

HELEN: Pretty close.

TOM: No, that's not...why would you say that? You just caught me off guard is all. Seriously.

HELEN: Anyway, I was just playing. Big people are jolly, remember?

TOM: ...Ummm-hmmm...

HELEN: It's one of our best qualities.

TOM: Well, at least you've got one.

HELEN: And you don't?

TOM: Ahhh...open for debate.

HELEN: Really?

TOM: I mean...you know, if I really had to come up with one, for, say, the big guy upstairs or whatever, I'd probably do something like, "does not run with scissors" or one of those. "Plays well with others."

HELEN: Really? Handsome guy like you and that's all you're good for...to look at?

TOM: Pretty much.

HELEN: Good to know. *(Opens a pudding)* You want one?

TOM: Nah, I shouldn't...

HELEN: Why?

TOM: Excellent question. Okay.

(TOM *takes a tub of rice pudding from* HELEN *and digs in.)*

HELEN: Good?

TOM: Mmmmmmm...wonderful. Haven't done that in ages.

HELEN: What?

TOM: Enjoyed myself. Like that. Put something in my mouth without reading the back label like some bible scholar...

(TOM *gives an example—holding the pudding up to the light as if it was an antiquity and squinting at it. Examining it from all angles. This makes her laugh again. A lot)*

TOM: Alright, O K, we're gonna have to ask you to leave...you're actually enjoying yourself during the work week.

HELEN: Right! Sorry...

TOM: No, It's O K, I told you, I love your laugh.

HELEN: Thanks. Again.

TOM: You're welcome...again.

HELEN: So...no other good qualities, huh?

TOM: Ahhhhh, I suppose. Faithful friend and co-worker, dependable, takes directions well.

HELEN: What about good lover? Not on the list?

(TOM *stares at* HELEN, *glances around. She keeps looking right at him.)*

TOM: That's very direct…

HELEN: Librarians are funny people.

TOM: I guess…I shouldn't've let my card lapse!

HELEN: So?

TOM: Ummm…I'm O K. I mean, no reports of absolute dissatisfaction, but I don't think I'm, like, Valentino or anything.

HELEN: He died really unhappy, though. I've read his biography.

TOM: One of the perks of the job…

HELEN: Right! I've read just about every biography in the place, actually. Real people interest me. I don't really have much time for fiction. "Fiction is for the weak and faint of heart." Somebody said that, a Frenchman, I think.

TOM: Cool…

HELEN: Anyway, you don't have to answer the question. It was rude.

TOM: No, I…I mean, I sort of did.

HELEN: And you're what? Just O K?

TOM: Something like that…I do fine! Wow. I've never…been asked that before. In that way.

HELEN: No?

TOM: Not at lunch, anyhow! *(Beat)* It's kind of invigorating, actually. You seem like a really…I don't know. An interesting person, I guess.

(They laugh together again. Really enjoying themselves)

HELEN: You should swing by the library some time. See what you've been missing…

TOM: Yeah. Listen, I'm…I need to get back to the office. Downtown. So I should finish up my, ahhh…

HELEN: 'Course. *(Beat)* Sorry if I was…

TOM: No, no, it was…but could we…. I don't know what I'm asking here. Should we see each other again?

HELEN: Why?

TOM: I dunno…I mean, I'm just, it'd be good, I think. You seem really nice and I'm…what can I say, I'm just asking….sort of outta the blue. So, could we? *(Beat)* I'm not trying to pick you up or anything, I just…

HELEN: Too bad. *(Smiles)* Yes. We should.

TOM: For lunch? Or, ummm, dinner…?

HELEN: I don't only eat. I can be coaxed into doing other stuff, too…

TOM: Of course! I didn't mean…

HELEN: I know. It's a joke.

TOM: Right, sure…I'm really striking out on the humor part here!

HELEN: You're doing fine… *(Beat)* So when?

TOM: Any time.

HELEN: How about Friday? I'm good for Fridays, my day off.

TOM: Ummm, yeah. Evening.

HELEN: Great. *(She reaches over and takes a pen out of TOM's shirt pocket and writes her number down on the edge of a napkin.)* …Now when you wipe your mouth you'll think of me.

TOM: Good plan. *(Beat)* So, ok, library lady, I'll call you…

HELEN: Helen. My name's "Helen".

TOM: As in "of Troy"? *(Groans)* That was so lame, sorry…

HELEN: Right, the thousand ships and all. But that was just so they could carry me back…

(TOM *stands there, thinking about this. Doesn't get it*)

HELEN: …because it would take that many to lift me… don't worry about it.

TOM: Oh, I see. *(Laughs)* I got it!

HELEN: Yeah. Just trying to be cute.

TOM: No, yes, I get it now…but you shouldn't do that, though. Make fun of yourself so much.

HELEN: Why not?

TOM: Ummmmmm…I'm sure there's a very good reason. I'll get back to you.

HELEN: You do that. You've got my number there…

TOM: Right. I'll call you. And I'm Tom, by the way.

HELEN: I'll see you. Tom.

(HELEN *wanders off with her tray and her bag.* TOM *stands alone. After a moment, she returns. Walks right up to the man and gets close.*)

HELEN: So, look, I figure there's every reason why I'll never hear from you again, and that's why I came back here…just to say that I don't do this, come after guys or anything, not like some regular habit or whatever, so I thought you should know that. I think you're really cute and nice and that sort of thing…you might have a girlfriend already or not be attracted to me, I would just totally understand that, I would, but I really do hope you call me. Just even to talk on the phone would be fine, because I'd like that, if we were only these phone buddies…I think I would. Just…don't be afraid, Tom, I guess that' s why I came back here to say that. Please do not let yourself be afraid of me or of taking some kind of blind chance, or what people think… because this could be so great.

(HELEN *smiles at* TOM *and does what she promised:*
wanders out of the joint. He watches her go, waves when she
nears the door.)

(TOM *goes back to eating the pudding and then looks up, off*
in the direction that she left in. He slowly folds the napkin
up and pockets it.)

"Back to business and under suspicion"

(TOM *at his place of work. Busy doing something. Another*
guy enters, carrying some files and a cup of coffee. He throws
himself down in a chair. His name is CARTER.)

CARTER: ...so you're not gonna tell me, right? Anything
else, I mean.

TOM: No, I'll...you know...

CARTER: Uh-uh, no you won't. I know you.

TOM: That's not true, I always tell you crap! All kinds
of crap about me.

CARTER: Yeah, but not the good stuff that I wanna hear.
The dirt.

TOM: I don't have dirt...

CARTER: Everybody's got dirt, my friend! We're dirty,
us folks. Very dirty.

TOM: Who's "us folks"?

CARTER: People. You and me-type people.

TOM: It's not...this is not some nasty thing that I'm
trying to keep from you. Seriously.

CARTER: ...O K then, so?

TOM: This is just...it's new, that's all. I don't know
what it is yet, so...

CARTER: So, like I said, you're not gonna tell me shit.

TOM: Kinda. Yeah.

CARTER: Fine. I don't care.

TOM: Bull…you're dying to hear.

CARTER: Yes, but I'll wait. I'll hire some private eye or whatnot, get the scoop that way. Whatever it takes.

TOM: Come on! I just wanna see what it is first, if it's worth talking to anyone about or not. What I will say right now is that I am very happy…

CARTER: O K, now you're frightening me…

TOM: What?

CARTER: I don't like it when you get all upbeat! Then it's like girlfriend city, and that's scary.

TOM: It's not scary…

CARTER: This is when we lose you for weeks at a time. Tom gets a lady friend and he drops off the map, I know how this one works…

TOM: I'm not at all like that!

CARTER: Yes, you are…

TOM: No, uh-uh. If anybody is, you are.

CARTER: Yeah, but that's for good reason. I'm actually having sex with them.

TOM: Very funny.

CARTER: Seriously.

TOM: Shut the hell up! I have sex…

CARTER: Uh-uh, "oral" doesn't count…and especially for someone who thinks it means talking a person to death.

TOM: Hooooo…funny! (*Beat*) Are you in here for an actual reason?

CARTER: I'm sure I had one when I started down the hall…

TOM: …Perfect…

CARTER: Oh, yeah, now I recall. Because I was bored in my office… *(Beat)* …plus, you have nicer windows.

TOM: Feel free to open one and jump…

CARTER: Tommy, you are so clever!

TOM: Seriously, though, I've got work.

CARTER: I've got work, too. We've all got work, Tom, that's why they call it that. "Work." Because that's what we do here.

TOM: I agree. And I want to get back to mine…

CARTER: Fine. *(Picks up a ball)* Dollar a point?

(TOM nods and the two men break into a lazy game of nerf "pig". The hoop hangs on the back of TOM's door.)

(A female co-worker [JEANNIE] walks in, carrying a stack of reports— ruins the game. She stops at TOM's desk and drops a few. Smiles. CARTER eyes her, then she speaks.)

JEANNIE: Hello. Morning, Tom…

TOM: Hey, Jeannie.

JEANNIE: Hi, *(Drops off muffin)* Snagged you the last muffin…

TOM: Oh, wow. *(Glances at CARTER)* Thanks.

JEANNIE: No prob.

CARTER: I'm sure mine's being toasted. *(Waits)* Kidding. Guess What?

JEANNIE: What?

CARTER: I said guess.

JEANNIE: Ummm…you're an asshole?

(TOM *giggles out loud at this one.* CARTER *blushes, then regroups.* JEANNIE *smiles over at* TOM.)

TOM: Aaah, you cheated! Somebody gave you the answers...

JEANNIE: Exactly!

CARTER: You guys are hilarious.

JEANNIE: What is it? I need to get back.

CARTER: O K, then don't worry about it.

JEANNIE: Just tell me. What?

CARTER: Need to know basis. Tom's got a gal.

TOM: Would you shut up!

CARTER: Word on the street...

TOM: Carter, seriously...

JEANNIE: Really? (*To* TOM) That's not true, right?

TOM: No...he's just being a dick.

CARTER: Am not! I mean, yes, I am a dick sometimes, but not at the moment.

JEANNIE: Tom...?

CARTER: He does.

TOM: I do not.

CARTER: It's what I heard...

TOM: Carter, knock it off. Jeannie, he's just trying to...

(JEANNIE *stands there for a bit longer, looking back and forth between* CARTER *and* TOM. *Finally she saunters out.*)

TOM: You prick.

CARTER: What?

TOM: That's not funny.

CARTER: It was pretty damn funny from over here...

TOM: I'm serious.

CARTER: Me, too. Try sitting on the couch and see if it's any funnier. *(He moves over.)* Plenty of room.

TOM: You know we've been dating…

CARTER: Of course. I-know-all.

TOM: I mean it. You know how she gets.

CARTER: Yes, I know… *(Beat)* Why do you think I said something? I'm not gonna tell the snack shop guy out front…I mean, why the fuck would he care?

TOM: You are a piece of work, you know that?

CARTER: I try. *(Beat)* Anyway, that's what you can expect, by the way. Mean-spirited shit like that until you tell me who she is.

TOM: I'm not gonna say a damn thing now…

CARTER: Your choice. But I'll find out, I promise…

TOM: Yeah, yeah…

CARTER: And then up goes her polaroid in the break room.

TOM: Fucker.

CARTER: Maybe. After you're through with her, of course…

TOM: Shut up and go back to your lair, Satan. Begone.

CARTER: Okay. *(Beat)* Hey, seriously though…does Jeannie look kind of soft to you?

TOM: What?

CARTER: A minute ago…doesn't she look a bit sloppy or something? In her ass, I'm saying. A couple of pounds.

TOM: …No…

CARTER: Come on, I'm just talking. It's not a judgment on you.

TOM: I know, but…I'm not obsessed by bodies the way you are. I'm not.

CARTER: I don't know what it is, but I was noticing yesterday. She came in to my office with her suit jacket off and had on one of those, you know, flimsy pair of slacks, with no seam up the rear and…I seriously think her backside isn't as taut as it used to be.

TOM: Dude, you need some help…

CARTER: What? It's an observation, that's all…her ass is right there. I can't help it if I observe things.

TOM: No, but you can keep it to your-self! And your therapist, who I hope you're still seeing…

CARTER: Nah, that shit was too expensive. Plus, she was a total bitch.

TOM: Nice.

CARTER: It's not, like, some derogatory thing I'm saying about her—not the therapist cunt, but Jeannie— it's just an idle thought. That's the problem with winter: chicks don't get out much and they bloat up…

TOM: O K, I really can't deal with you right now, so… go.

CARTER: Whatever. We on for basketball tomorrow? Chad can't make it any other time…

TOM: Ahh, yeah. But after nine, O K? I've got a dinner thing.

(*Off of* CARTER'*s look*)

TOM: For work, dumb-shit.

CARTER: Sure.

TOM: It is! I've got those folks from the, ahhh… you know…

CARTER: No, what?

TOM: The Chicago group is coming into town. *(Beat)* They are...

CARTER: Cool. I'll email the other guys and meet you at the Y. See ya.

(CARTER finally gets up and saunters over to TOM—a quick "high-five" and CARTER exits. TOM returns to his work as CARTER looks back inside the room.)

CARTER: I'm swinging past the restaurant to check, so you better be telling the truth...

TOM: Asshole.

CARTER: That's me. But when I get my PhD it'll be Doctor Asshole, so, hey. Something to look forward to...

(He is gone. TOM shakes his head and gets back to the files that JEANNIE has left. A minute later he looks up to see her standing in his doorway.)

JEANNIE: Hey. *(Smiles)*

TOM: Oh, hi. There.

JEANNIE: Got a minute?

TOM: Sure.

JEANNIE: I forgot some.... *(Holds up an extra file)* Forgot this one.

TOM: Ah. Thanks.

JEANNIE: Oh, I, umm, I went on Ticket-Master and they still have those Coldplay seats, so...

TOM: Really? Orchestra?

JEANNIE: Uh-huh, yeah. A few pairs...

TOM: Huh. I thought I checked all the...maybe they... hmmm. *(Beat)* Cool. I'll...

(TOM gets up and crosses to JEANNIE, reaching for the folder. She holds it a moment and they both tug on it.)

JEANNIE: So…is it true, what he said?

TOM: Who, Carter?

JEANNIE: Yeah.

TOM: Ummm…

JEANNIE: Oh. *(Beat)* So where does that put us, then? I mean, I thought…

TOM: No, I'm not saying it's…he's an idiot, so, you know, you have to make some allowances.

JEANNIE: Right. *(Grins)* That's true…

TOM: But…I don't know what I'm doing. You know that. I'm…

JEANNIE: Yes, I do. All while we've been going out I could tell that, but I still liked you. Gave you a million or so chances, but…hey. Whatever.

TOM: I know that, Jeannie, I know, I'm just…it's complicated.

JEANNIE: I'm not saying that I'm some, you know, beauty queen, but guys do like me. They really, really do.

TOM: I know, come on…please. I like you. Don't say it like that.

JEANNIE: Yeah, well…I wish you'd fire up a signal flare every now and then. *(Smiles)* Could use it over here…

TOM: Sorry. I do, though…

JEANNIE: Doesn't seem like it. I mean, I've tried sweet and forceful and, you know, nonchalant. Everything. I don't get it. What do you want me to do here?

TOM: Nothing. I'm…

JEANNIE: What? *(Beat)* So, just tell me. Is he lying or not?

TOM: Carter is...I mean, by nature he's a liar. You know that. He likes to provoke people. Get 'em riled up.

JEANNIE: ...Which says nothing.

TOM: Jeannie, come on...

JEANNIE: So you are.

TOM: I'm not...no. I'm not "seeing" any other person, alright? Promise.

JEANNIE: Look, I'm just asking, so don't make it seem like I'm pulling on your eye teeth or something. If you don't wanna tell me, then O K.

TOM: I'm saying it, to you, right now.

JEANNIE: Yeah, but...

TOM: Carter's an ass. He's...

JEANNIE: ...So why do you hang out with him then? Huh? All those guys down in Development. *(Beat)* Why?

TOM: Because...I'm needy and shallow. *(Smiles)* Hell, I dunno! Because we all started out here together and it's, you know, it's easier to go along sometimes, to just hang out and not make, like, some big tsunami or that kinda thing. I know it's dumb, but...he's funny. He doesn't bug me that much.

JEANNIE: Obviously.

TOM: Jeannie, come on, don't be...he's just playing around.

JEANNIE: So, nobody then?

TOM: I didn't...because...I'm not saying that I'm... what?

JEANNIE: Don't do your circles thing, O K? Do not do that...

TOM: What're you even…?

JEANNIE: Talking around shit, that's what I'm saying. I hate that! Are-you-dating-someone?

TOM: No. Kind of. Hell, I dunno! I'm… It's not some big thing.

JEANNIE: I see.

TOM: Look, We agreed that we should be able to…I'm not doing anything, like, wrong.

JEANNIE: But you're pretty defensive about it.

TOM: Yeah, because…because you get all…you know how you are.

JEANNIE: I'm not anything. Except confused. By a guy who tells me that he's interested in me. "Very," in fact, was the word he used. "I am very interested in you." And we date and then we stop and then he sends me stuff, like flowers and letters and keeps calling and wants to do it again, to try one more time, he tells me….but then we do not go out. We see each other at work but he keeps putting off the next date because of…God, I couldn't begin to list all of the excuses because it's Monday afternoon and I would probably be here, like, through the weekend. But now I hear he's met someone, a someone that he has managed—even with his many work obligations and boys' nights out and all his other related juvenile crap—he has some-how squeezed yet another person onto his social calendar.

(JEANNIE *edges a bit closer to* TOM *now. He steps back.*)

TOM: …See? This is what I was talking about.

JEANNIE: No, this is what I'm talking about right now! The bullshit you do to me and expect me to keep crawling back in here and taking it.

TOM: …I don't…want you to…

JEANNIE: Oh, so now you don't want me here? Is that it? Go ahead, then, say it. Go on. Say-it.

TOM: No, Jeannie, Jesus, can we just…I'd like to talk about this, but not in public. Alright?

(Off of JEANNIE'*s look)*

TOM: I mean, can we…maybe…

JEANNIE: You can "maybe" kiss my ass, Tom, and that's a definite maybe. You can pencil that one in your planner right now, O K?

(JEANNIE *turns abruptly and walks out. Before* TOM *can even react she is back. standing in the doorway.)*

TOM: …Jeannie, please. Let's…

JEANNIE: I can't wait to meet her. Really, I can't. *(Holds out file)* Here. I forgot to give you this…

(TOM *moves apprehensively toward the door.* JEANNIE *drops the file onto the floor and stalks off.)*

"A surprising night out together"

(TOM *and* HELEN *sitting at a table in a cozy restaurant. a meal spread out before them.* TOM *is chowing down on exotic cuisine;* HELEN *is a bit more hesitant.)*

TOM: …go on, jump in there! *(Prompts her)* Be brave.

HELEN: You're absolutely sure it's dead, right? Because if it's just holding its breath, then I'm…

TOM: Yeah! *(Laughs)* Definitely…

HELEN: O K. *(Looks again)* Positive?

TOM: Well, I wasn't back there watching 'em fix it but, yeah, in theory.

HELEN: I mean, I'm pretty adventurous, but, you know…

TOM: No, I'm the same way. It's…I'm not big on swallowing anything I saw on Discovery Channel either, believe me… *(Smiles)* It's good. Promise.

(HELEN *smiles and nods, gobbles something down with her eyes closed. Happy with the results.* TOM *smiles as he eats something, too. Lets a moment of silence hang)*

TOM: …Can I ask you something?

HELEN: No. I'm kidding. Sure, what?

TOM: I meant to ask you this the other night…I mean, when we went to that martini bar… *(Beat)* You love war movies?

(HELEN *smiles over at* TOM *and nods. Says nothing else)*

TOM: Okay, first obvious question. Why?

HELEN: Just because.

TOM: Not fair! That's not an answer…

HELEN: Yes, it is.

TOM: But not a good one. One that tells me anything about you…

HELEN: Ohhh, I see. You're gonna dig deep now, is that it?

TOM: Something like that…little Freud action.

HELEN: Oh, Freud, huh?

TOM: I figured you read his biography.

HELEN: Yes, I have. *(Beat)* I like war movies because of all the big…long gun barrels.

(*This makes* TOM *laugh and he reaches out for* HELEN's *hand. He grabs it and squeezes, holding on to it. She notices.*)

TOM: Come on! Seriously…

HELEN: O K, O K…I'm… *(Beat)* You have my hand there, you know.

TOM: Yeah, I…is that not…?

HELEN: It's fine. Just wanted to ask and see if it was an accident or not.

TOM: Umm…no. It wasn't, no. But…now you're making me self-conscious.

(TOM *looks around the restaurant.* HELEN *notices this, too.*)

TOM: I want to….hold it, I mean, if that's O K.

HELEN: Of course.

TOM: Good.

(HELEN *and* TOM *sit and stare at one another for a moment. Silence*)

HELEN: I would like to have a bit more of my tuna later…but I can wait.

TOM: Sorry! Shit…

HELEN: I'm kidding you.

(TOM *looks at* HELEN, *then pulls away. Embarrassed. He points at her food.*)

TOM: No, you should…that's fine. We can do that after, or walking back to the car or something. We should eat. Yes.

HELEN: Tom…I really was joking.

TOM: I know, but… (*He eats.*) I'm ready for some of mine, too.

(HELEN *and* TOM *both take a bite or two, laughing across the table.*)

TOM: So, seriously…what's the deal on the war flicks? You know way too many of those things to've just been reading the *T V Guide* or that kind of thing…

HELEN: Please, I'm a professional.

TOM: Oh, yeah? Prove it.

HELEN: Let's see if you can keep up. Von Ryan's... Come on, little quiz...Von Ryan's...

TOM: ...Train...no, wait...Express!

HELEN: Lonely are the...

TOM: Brave.

HELEN: Porkchop...

TOM: ...Hill.

HELEN: Kelly's...

TOM: ...Heroes.

HELEN: Aces...

TOM: ...High.

HELEN: Alright, a little bonus round here. Heaven Knows, Mr....

TOM: Magoo!

HELEN: No, Allison.

TOM: Jesus...and most of those are obscure, too!

HELEN: I know. *(Beat)* I work in audio/visual.

TOM: Well, you're very....except that one.

HELEN: Which?

TOM: *Lonely Are The Brave.*

HELEN: It's a...what?

TOM: A western. Sort of. With Kirk Douglas.

HELEN: Oh, right, no, I mean...is it?

TOM: Yeah. You know, with him on the horse and he's being chased by, like, guys in helicopters and stuff? It's that one. It's really good, but, yeah. Western.

HELEN: Huh. *(Considers)* Oh, right, right, yes, I've seen it, black and white right? But I'm getting the name confused. I mean *None But the Brave.* The Frank Sinatra one. On that atoll in the Pacific…

TOM: You're…nobody's seen that one! Alright, this is now, like, an officially quirky side of you. *(Grins)* "Atoll"?

HELEN: Hey, I'm a librarian…

TOM: Uh-uh. "Printed word specialist."

HELEN: Right! *(Laughs)* Anyway, I grew up with 'em, that's all. I have three brothers, plus my dad. They were on all the time, and so I watched a lot of them, or parts of 'em, anyway. All growing up.

TOM: Yeah, me too. I mean, that same scenario. What is it about fathers and those movies? *(Beat)* He also directed that one, too.

HELEN: Your father?

TOM: No…Sinatra! You're funny.

HELEN: Thanks.

TOM: I mean, jolly.

(HELEN *and* TOM *both laugh again. Really enjoying each other now.)*

TOM: But, seriously, I wonder. Why?

HELEN: Well…most of them either fought in wars or wanted to, or had some relative who did or whatever. Or they just like watching other guys get shot, that could be it, too.

TOM: Probably right!

HELEN: I'm not joking. I think guys today feel left out, like, guilty about not having to kill things, provide food. All that "Early Man" stuff. *(Beat)* But for me…I just enjoyed being around my family. Sitting on the couch, big bowl of popcorn. It felt good.

TOM: …Right…

HELEN: And it saved me the embarrassment of waiting around for boys to call me up.

TOM: What do you mean?

HELEN: Ummm, you probably couldn't guess, but I didn't date a lot when I was in school.

TOM: Oh.

HELEN: *(Whispers)* ...I used to be a little heavy.

(HELEN *chuckles.* TOM *joins in half-heartedly, then stops.*)

TOM: Huh. *(Beat)* And is that...is it alright to talk about...I dunno, your weight and everything, or should I...?

HELEN: No, go ahead. It's not a shame thing for me. Not any more.

TOM: "Any more"?

HELEN: Well...it's all shame when you're younger, isn't it? You hate how you look or sound or, you know, all that stuff that we go through. As kids. But I'm pretty alright with who I am now. The trick is getting other people to be O K with it!

TOM: Right. And, so...have you always been, like...you know?

HELEN: No. What?

TOM: Ummm, big...boned, or whatever.

(HELEN *laughs out loud at this one. Another beauty, which makes* TOM *giggle along. She takes his hand this time.*)

HELEN: That was kind of precious. One of my favorites, actually...

TOM: What?

HELEN: "Big-boned." My dad used to throw that one around, too.

TOM: Well...I'm just trying to be...

HELEN: Don't. Not for me. I just want you to be truthful, O K? Seriously.

TOM: Alright.

HELEN: However things end up here—and I have high hopes, but— *(Smiles)* I want you to be honest with me.

TOM: …I can do that. Promise.

HELEN: Good. Great. Fair enough.

TOM: So, then, ummm…I don't know what to say here exactly, but… *(Beat)* …Helen, I like your body…what I imagine your body to be. It's…

HELEN: Tom, It's O K…I'm not worried about it. I mean, you would not be here next to me, if you didn't want to be. Right?

TOM: Sure. Yes.

HELEN: So, then…I'm good. Secure about it. Truthfully. I know that you're here because you like me. A little bit, anyway.

TOM: That's true. I do, yes. Like you.

HELEN: Then good… *(Smiles)* So, why don't we finish up our seafood… *(Thinks)* …stuff. What's this called again?

TOM: Ahh…you got the, umm, "Yellowfin Tartare" and I got their, I don't remember now. "Spicy Kimchi", maybe? With crab…

HELEN: Yeah, that was it.

(HELEN Smiles and touches TOM's hand again, then goes back to eating. He watches her as she takes a few more bites.)

TOM: How's your meal? O K?

HELEN: Delicious, actually. Little bit of ginger and scallions, I like it…

TOM: Good. *(Beat)* You know, the yellowfin is traditionally the "biggest boned" of the tuna family...

HELEN: Oh really? *(Giggles)* Tell me more.

TOM: Seriously—with a hearty, heavy flavor...

(HELEN and TOM laugh together, their heads coming in close contact. Suddenly, she notices that he is now staring off, behind her. She swings around and spots CARTER, a drink in one hand. TOM awkwardly stands up.)

TOM: Hey...

CARTER: Well, hello there.

TOM: Carter, this is...Helen, I'd like you to meet my... this is Carter, who works with us. I mean, me.

(HELEN smiles and holds a hand up. CARTER takes it and shakes it. Looks around)

CARTER: Where's the rest of 'em? Late?

(An uncomfortable moment hangs in the air. HELEN begins to stand.)

HELEN: I'm going to use the little girl's room. Even though I hate the term.

TOM: Right! *(Tries to laugh)* Me, too.

CARTER: Well, it's better than "shitter".

HELEN: Very true. *(Beat)* Great to meet you, Carter.

CARTER: Yeah, you too.

(HELEN walks off and CARTER watches her go—all the way off. he then turns to TOM and gestures.)

CARTER: ...I hope it's twins. *(Smiles)* Bet you're glad you promised to play basketball tonight, huh?

TOM: ...Uh-huh.

CARTER: What the hell is that?

TOM: I just told you. Her name's Helen and she's...you know...

CARTER: ...And how come the others aren't here?

TOM: Because we're...I mean...

(CARTER *reaches over and pokes at* TOM'S *sweater. Giggles*)

CARTER: Jesus....nice sweater there, bub. You join the P G A or something?

TOM: Very funny! I'm not...

CARTER: ...They didn't just send her, did they? Not that she couldn't eat for five...

TOM: Carter, don't say stuff like that. It's not nice.

CARTER: I know that. I wasn't being nice. That was me being honest.

TOM: Seriously, though...

CARTER: Hey, she's not here, ok, so can you ease up on the Knights of the Round Table shit? She's off to the bathroom... *(Beat)* With a basket of dinner rolls hidden under her skirt, if I'm not mistaken...

TOM: Can you please...? Jesus.

CARTER: O K, alright! God, you are really just not fun at all when you're out with a woman, you know that? Even some beast from work...

TOM: She's not...just leave her alone.

CARTER: Fine. *(Beat)* You gonna be there by nine? Howard's gotta hit the road by eleven-thirty...

TOM: Yes, you know that...yes. *(Looking around)* Why are you here?

CARTER: I told you I was coming by.

TOM: Yeah, but how'd you know where...?

CARTER: Because you always come here! But Tom? This place is kinda out-of- the-loop, I hate to tell you. By, like, ahh, three years.

TOM: Yeah, well, I like it. *(Beat)* So, can I just finish up and...do you mind?

CARTER: No, whatever. Just checking on ya.

TOM: Fine.

CARTER: Thought I might catch you with...you know. Her.

TOM: You really are an ass...

CARTER: Pretty much. But, surprisingly, it doesn't give me a big head...

TOM: Will you just please go?! Come on.

CARTER: Fine, fine. See you at nine.

TOM: Yeah. See you.

(CARTER takes another gulp from his drink, then stops. He starts off but leans in close to TOM.)

CARTER: Dude...I so wish I would've caught you with her! Damn it. Anyway...

(At that moment, HELEN returns and stands next to CARTER. He pulls out her chair and seats her.)

HELEN: Thank you...

CARTER: Pleasure. *(To HELEN)* And don't let this cheap-skate stiff you on the dessert! They've got a hell of a green tea ice cream here...

HELEN: ...Good to know...

TOM: See you later, Carter.

HELEN: Goodbye. Nice to meet you.

CARTER: You too, ummm...what was it again?

HELEN: "Helen."

CARTER: Right. *(Over his shoulder)* And say "hello" to the Windy City for me!

(CARTER is gone. TOM watches him go and then turns back to HELEN. Tries to smile)

HELEN: …What does that mean?

TOM: He's…you know, he's a…

HELEN: …Why would he think I'm from Chicago?

TOM: He doesn't. No. That was for me. To me. I'm… going there for work.

HELEN: You are?

TOM: For, like, yeah. Just a day or two next week. Business.

HELEN: Oh. I see…really?

TOM: Yep. I was gonna tell you, but then we got to talking, is all.

HELEN: Right. *(Beat)* He seems O K. Nice. And he works with you?

TOM: Uh-huh. Down the hall. I mean, not with me, but…I see him around. *(Beat)* He's not going to Chicago. Just me.

HELEN: Got it. *(Beat)* …did I mention my second interview that I got? It's for that…I did, didn't I? Yeah.

(HELEN and TOM both return to eating their meals. Silence. A long one, in fact. Finally, he stops and looks at her.)

TOM: …I know that you know. I mean, I can tell. That you do. I made a…he thinks that this is, like, a business dinner and I didn't say anything.

HELEN: O K.

TOM: No, its not O K. So, I want you to know that I'm sorry. I am. He really just surprised me and I got all…

HELEN: I understand.

TOM: I did wanna say something but I'm, I…I didn't.

HELEN: At least you're honest.

TOM: -ish.

HELEN: It's something to work on then, right?

TOM: …Yeah. That's true.

(HELEN *reaches over and gives* TOM *a kiss on the mouth. He responds and the moment grows in intensity.*)

"The work friends figure it out"

(TOM *at his desk, working.* CARTER *sprawled on a couch and reading a magazine. He holds up a photo for* TOM *to look at. They both smile.*)

(*After a moment,* JEANNIE *appears in the doorway. Silently staring over at* TOM)

CARTER: Hey, Jeannie. What's up?

JEANNIE: Hi. (*To* CARTER) Gee, you're in here and not working. That comes as quite a shock…

CARTER: You so dig me.

JEANNIE: Oh God. Tom?

(JEANNIE *is done with* CARTER *and turns to* TOM. *Stares*)

TOM: What? Good morning, by the way…

JEANNIE: Good morning. How's things?

TOM: You know. O K.

JEANNIE: I'll bet. I will just bet. (*Beat*) Carter, can you give us a minute?

CARTER: Not if this is gonna get good… (*To* TOM) Do you want me to go?

JEANNIE: Please…

TOM: I don't…I'm not afraid of us talking in front of him. He'll find out, anyway.

CARTER: Exactly! I promise not to say a word.

JEANNIE: Yeah, just print a story in the newsletter…

CARTER: Well, I gotta get it out somehow.

(CARTER *laughs but no one joins in. He sputters out and sits back.*)

JEANNIE: Fine. Whatever.

TOM: Seriously…Jeannie, if you wanna say something to me, go ahead. *(He stands up.)* That's fine.

JEANNIE: Then why're you standing?

TOM: What? Oh, you know, just…I felt like stretching.

(CARTER *laughs.* JEANNIE *glances over at him—he smiles and mimes zipping his mouth shut. She turns back to* TOM.)

JEANNIE: You know I'm in accounting, right? You do know that.

TOM: Of course.

JEANNIE: So anything you turn in is going to come past me, I mean, over my desk. True?

TOM: I guess…

JEANNIE: No, you know it. I know that you know because I've had you come in there, to my office, looking for stuff before. *(To* CARTER*)* Quit looking at my ass. An old receipt or some stack of files. I mean, it's how we first got to be…

TOM: No, you're right. That's true…

JEANNIE: We met that way so I'm sure you realize just how these things go. The course they take. You turn in your expense reports, attach the receipts and write in the little explanations and we do the rest. You know all this.

TOM: Yeah, Jeannie, I get it. I mean, I know how to do that. So...?

JEANNIE: ...I waited for your big Chicago dinner to come through, just so I could see. I heard Carter joking around about it and so I wanted to, you know, check out who you were with. *(Beat)* But nothing has been turned in yet. Why's that? Because you've always been—how can I put this? —pretty damn anal about it before.

(TOM doesn't say anything, glancing over at CARTER.)

CARTER: ...One quick interjection? It was just an off-handed comment, that's all.

JEANNIE: Just shut up, O K?

CARTER: I'm done.

JEANNIE: *(Turns)* So...Tom? What's up?

TOM: Nothing. Jesus, I mean...

JEANNIE: I'm just curious. But it's also my business, so, you know...

TOM: What, to, like, stalk me?

JEANNIE: Please, you wish...to keep up on how people are utilizing their expense accounts, shit like that.

TOM: So, what? You're busting me for not asking to be reimbursed?

JEANNIE: No...I'm keeping things straight. Alright? It's my job.

TOM: Yeah, but I bet you're not...you know, down at everybody's office, going through all their...

JEANNIE: Yes, I am, as a matter of fact. I stay here late almost every night, digging through mountains of crap that you guys spend out there on the road and in restaurants and at your little luxury hotels, so it's not just you. Alright? Please do not flatter yourself...

TOM: Whatever.

JEANNIE: Yeah, "whatever". That's exactly what I'm asking. "Hey, `whatever' happened to that Chicago dinner that Tom supposedly went on?"

(JEANNIE *finishes and waits.* CARTER *sits up, interested.*)

TOM: I...I guess I must've forgot.

JEANNIE: To what?

TOM: To turn in the report! God. My receipts and stuff. I'll...I can staple it to next month's, right?

JEANNIE: You could. Or I can take it from you now, if you want.

TOM: No, I'm...I've got it all back at my apartment, so...later's fine.

JEANNIE: It was a business dinner, right? With the guys from Chicago.

TOM: ...Yes.

CARTER: It's what he told me.

TOM: Carter.

CARTER: *(Holds up a hand)* Sorry...

TOM: I mean, not with the "guys", per se, but this woman. One woman who came in from...yeah. A woman.

CARTER: "Helen", I believe. *(Looks at* TOM*)* What? I'm just being helpful...

TOM: Yeah, thanks. *(To* JEANNIE*)* She was in town and we sat down and had a meal and talked over the, I mean, some of the...accounts from there. Like AmTel and...others.

JEANNIE: I see. Fine.

TOM: Alright? Can we put the hot tongs away now, or was there some more stuff that you wanted to...?

(TOM *tries to laugh and* CARTER *joins in.* JEANNIE *stares.*)

JEANNIE: Carter, can you please leave us alone for a second? Please.

CARTER: Tom?

TOM: No, Jeannie, shit…this is my office and he can… what is up with you?!

JEANNIE: God, fine. Whatever you want…you scared or something?

TOM: Ummmm…maybe. Yeah. I wouldn't exactly want you handling a butcher knife right now or anything…

(CARTER *laughs again, which makes* TOM *giggle a bit.*)

JEANNIE: Chicago doesn't have a record of anybody coming here last month. No one. No employee—man, woman. Fat chick. Nothing. I verified.

TOM: …You called Chicago?

JEANNIE: I did, yes.

TOM: Jeannie, I mean, shit…that is…that's, like, so…

JEANNIE: …Within my job description.

TOM: No, that goes beyond your…I mean let's be honest here, you are… being a little nuts about this!

JEANNIE: If I am, you made me that way.

TOM: I didn't do… (*To* CARTER) Dude, back me up here.

CARTER: Yeah, I gotta say…

(CARTER *starts to speak but* JEANNIE *cuts him off.*)

JEANNIE: Shh! So I found it odd—especially when I had to maneuver around the weight issue, trying to describe her from what Carter had said—and I'm just drawing blanks from this woman over the phone who's probably thinking I'm some crazy person but I have all the right information and the clearances and so she's accessing a bunch of these personnel records but, uh-uh, nothing. Not a single flight booked here in over three months. So—I slapped one of those little Post-it flags on it and came down here to ask you about the thing. Maybe you can help me out.

(TOM *looks over at* CARTER, *who holds up a finger.*)

CARTER: ...I never said "fat".

JEANNIE: Carter, you told me she was huge.

CARTER: Yeah, which is totally different. Shaq is huge, but nobody says the guy's fat...

JEANNIE: You said she was a pig!

CARTER: I don't think we should get off on a tangent here... *(To* TOM*)* I mean, Tom, you're the one who said she was in from Chicago.

TOM: No...

CARTER: You didn't?

TOM: No, I was...you inferred that...

CARTER: Yeah, because you told me you were having dinner with the...so, was she or not?

JEANNIE: That's really the question, isn't it? *(Beat)* Tom.

TOM: She was...yes, I was having dinner with one of our, she's a colleague from Chicago, but from one of our subsidiary suppliers...
I should've been clear about the...her...

CARTER: The name was "Helen", I believe.

TOM: Right, "Helen". About Helen's trip to...to see us.

JEANNIE: Tom.

TOM: I mean, not "see" us, no, she wasn't just dropping in, like checking up on us or anything, but she came here to explain some...several...new...options for our involvement in a, a, variety of...stuff.

JEANNIE: Tom…Tom, listen to yourself. Stop! You are, like, the worst liar ever. I mean it. In history.

TOM: Fine. Whatever you say.

(TOM *sits again, frustrated.* JEANNIE *approaches him.*)

TOM: What?

JEANNIE: Ummm…just the obvious stuff. Who-was-it?

TOM: She's a…just this girl.

JEANNIE: Excuse me?

TOM: Woman, then! I dunno. You know I mean "woman". A woman I met. She's someone that I've… who I took out, just got talking to at lunch one time and I was…yeah.

(JEANNIE *is lost for words.* CARTER *is connecting the dots.*)

JEANNIE: I see. And, so, she's…?

CARTER: Oh…shit. Fuck! Are you fucking kidding me?! HOLY SHIT!! (*He realizes he is being loud and gets up, crosses to the door and shuts it. Smiling broadly*) Dude… (*To* TOM) This is not her. You gotta tell me, tell me that much. This is not the…her her. Is it?

TOM: …Yeah. (*Beat*) Yes, Carter.

CARTER: Oh-my-God. Oh-my…

TOM: Just stop, ok?

CARTER: I mean…OH-MY-GOD! This is a…Jesus Christ!! She's…I gotta tell somebody

TOM: Would you just get out of here?!

JEANNIE: Fine, Tom, I'll go.

TOM: Not you Jeannie.

CARTER: Yeah, I gotta go find my camera. "Tommy Joins the Circus!"

TOM: Asshole.

CARTER: Oh, come on, man! You'd be doing the same thing to me…

TOM: Bullshit…

CARTER: That's a lie and you know it! You totally would…

TOM: No, I wouldn't. Nope. *(Beat)* We mess around a lot but I do not make fun of your…you know…

JEANNIE: So…you are seeing her, then.

TOM: It's not, no, but why do I have to discuss this?! Come on people we're at work here.

JEANNIE: Sure, fine, but if you wanna stop and talk about the Lakers for two hours with the guys, that'd be O K, right? Yeah, that's cool, but if I come in here because I'm trying to figure out just what the hell is going on in my relationship, well, that's something we better talk about later. Let's save that for some later time. Yeah, that's pretty fair!

TOM: We don't have a relationship!!

JEANNIE: Oh, really?!

TOM: Newsflash: No, we don't…I'm sorry, but you keep saying that, and I'm….you know…I keep trying to tell you that I'm not…this isn't…

JEANNIE: You said you wanted to try again! YOU told me that!!

TOM: To keep you from nagging at me!! Just to stop you from calling and going on and on and on about this all the time!! That's why!!!

JEANNIE: …oh.

TOM: O K? I mean, God…

JEANNIE: I see.

TOM: I'm sorry, but…I just don't…

JEANNIE: Then fine. Good.

(JEANNIE *suddenly reaches across the desk and smacks* TOM *across the face. Hard with an open palm. He stumbles back and hits his chair, which rolls out from under him.*)

(JEANNIE *walks to the door, swings it open wide. Before she goes, however, she turns back to* CARTER *and pushes him hard against the couch. She exits, slamming the door behind her.*)

(TOM *crosses to the door, opens it. Looks out. Holds up a hand to someone down the hall. Closes the door again*)

CARTER: ...I think she took that pretty well.

TOM: You dick.

CARTER: Hey, don't blame this shit on me.

TOM: I'm not, I just...damn it! Why do we even have to do this crap? Get all involved with people and...?

CARTER: Because we're clingy. It's what makes us different than the rest of the animals...

TOM: Yeah, thanks, that really helps.

CARTER: I do what I can...

(TOM *sits back down in his chair and* CARTER *plops back on the couch. They sit in silence for a moment.*)

CARTER: Hey...

TOM: What?

CARTER: This isn't meant as a...you know, to make up for what I said or whatnot, but in the spirit of full disclosure...my mom was fat. Is. As we speak.

TOM: ...That's great.

CARTER: No, I'm just saying...I know what it's like, I mean, why you were so embarrassed or...

TOM: I wasn't! I just...hell. I dunno. I sorta froze and, and then...

CARTER: ...dude, I understand. Like, totally. *(Beat)* I
used to walk ahead of her in the mall or, you know,
not tell her about stuff at school so there wouldn't
be, whatever. My own mom. I mean...I'm fifteen
and worried about every little thing and I've got this
fucking Sumo wrestler in a housecoat trailing around
behind me. That's about as bad as it can get! I'm not
kidding you. And the thing was, I blamed her for it.
I mean, it wasn't a disease or like some people have,
thyroid or that type of deal...she just shoveled shit into
her mouth all the time, had a few kids and, bang, she's
up there at three-fifty, maybe more. It used to seriously
piss me off. My dad was always working late...golfing
on weekends and I knew it was because of her. It had
to be! How's he gonna love something that looks like
that, get all fucking sexy with her? I'm just a kid at the
time, but I can remember thinking that.

TOM: ...God, that's...

*(CARTER waves this off, drifting in his own thoughts for a
moment.)*

CARTER: Yeah, it's whatever, but...this once, in the
grocery store, we're at an Albertson's and pushing four
baskets around—you wanna know how humiliating
that shit is?—and I'm supposed to be at a game by
seven, I'm on J V, and she's just farting around in the
candy aisle, picking up bags of "fun-size" Snickers and
checking out the calories. Yeah. I mean, can you believe
that?! So, I suddenly go off on her, like, this sophomore
in high school but I'm all screaming in her face...
don't look at the package, take a look in the fucking
mirror, you cow!! PUT 'EM DOWN! Holy shit, there's
stock boys—bunch of guys I know, even—are running
down the aisle. Manager stumbling out of his glass
booth there, the works. *(Beat)* But you know what? She
doesn't say a word about it. Ever. About the swearing,
the things I called her, nothing. Just this, like, one tear

I see…as we're sitting at a stoplight on the way home. That's all.

TOM: Wow. I'm, I mean…

CARTER: I did feel that way, though. Maybe I shouldn't've yelled or…but it was true, what I said. You don't like being fat, there's a pretty easy remedy, most times. Do-not-jam-so-much-food-down-your-fucking-gullet! *(Beat)* It's not that hard.

TOM: Right. I guess that's true. *(Beat)* It's confusing, though, the…

CARTER: What?

TOM: I dunno, I'm, like…I mean, that night, when you saw us? Why didn't I just come clean, say that I was having dinner, out with a friend even, instead of making all that shit up?

CARTER: …Because you're a pussy.

TOM: …Man, come on…

CARTER: No, I say that in the best way. We all are—guys, I mean—if it comes right down to it. Very rare is the dude who stands up for the shit he believes in…

TOM: I know! I wanna be better at that sorta stuff, but a lot of the time I'm just…yeah. A big wuss and I hate that! Despise that about me, but God, it's… No. I'm gonna work on it, I'll…I'll…

CARTER: Dude, relax, take a breath, don't hurt yourself…we can't all be Thomas More. And anyway, look what happened to him! Poor bastard…

TOM: True. *(Beat)* No offense, but how the hell do you know about Thomas More?

CARTER: Hey…I only cheated off the top two percentile in my class.

(TOM nods and drifts. CARTER does the same. Silence)

TOM: ...Geez, I wish Jeannie wasn't so, you know. Damn.

CARTER: She's pissed. I mean, nobody likes getting screwed around.

TOM: I didn't... *(Beat)* You think this is how I wanted it to end up? Huh?

CARTER: No...but it's the way these things usually do.

TOM: I guess.

CARTER: I know. The guy who first thought up the whole "I hope we can still be friends" thing must be giggling his dick off somewhere...

TOM: Probably. *(Beat)* You think maybe I should go down there and talk to her? Just...

CARTER: Oh, yeah, that's a good idea. Meet her on her turf...with all those accounting chicks around. Perfect.

TOM: I don't want her all mad, though. Maybe just an e-mail...

CARTER: Yeah, with one of those smiley- faced icons or something. Come on, be serious!

TOM: What?

CARTER: It's over. You are so done...

TOM: I know. I'm not saying to try and salvage anything, but just so that we can...shit, I dunno! We have to work together, so...

CARTER: It's the way of the world. Break ups are ugly. I mean, unless you get to watch 'em from over here. *(Laughs)* She so nailed you!

TOM: Come on, Carter, don't.

CARTER: I'm sorry, but it was awesome. I mean, I've seen you get tagged by some bad boys playing ball, never even budge—and this little girl walks in and takes you out like Sonny Liston...BAM!! Pretty cool.

TOM: Yeah, hilarious. *(Beat)* Maybe I'll just send her a quick one...

(CARTER *waves him off and picks up another magazine.* TOM *quickly types something on his computer and hits a button to send it off.)*

TOM: ...it can't hurt.

CARTER: Not as much as your face, anyway.

(CARTER *and* TOM *sit and stare at one another for a moment. Silence)*

CARTER: ...You got a photo? Of her.

TOM: You are not getting a picture. Not even a peek...

CARTER: I will not take it. I promise.

TOM: Uh-huh. Sure.

CARTER: I won't! I just wanna see her one more time.

TOM: Man, you are so...I don't even get why I like you.

CARTER: Because you're like me.

TOM: No, I'm not.

CARTER: You so are! Absolutely.

TOM: That's not true. *(Grins)* No.

CARTER: Right. *(Beat)* You do that little boy thing, "Oh, I'm so innocent" trick that women eat up but you are so much like me it's not even funny. Seriously...

TOM: Carter, that's not at all...

CARTER: Bullshit! You laugh at the same jokes and check out the same asses that I do, you date all these gals and act like you're Mister Sensitive but how does it always end up? The exact same way is does for me... you get bored or cornered or feel a touch nervous and you drop 'em like they were old produce. Every time. Dude, I'm not blind...

TOM: Yeah, but that's because, I mean, with Jeannie it's been...you know.

CARTER: I'm not talking about just her. I mean with anybody. Since I've know you. There's no shame in it...it's not very nice, but I don't think we were put down here to be nice. Not exclusively, anyway. Every so often we sprinkle a little "nice" in on top, just to keep 'em guessing, but...that's about it.

TOM: You scare me a little...I mean it.

CARTER: Ahh, it's just Tuesday. Tuesday's suck...

(CARTER *and* TOM *sit back down and contemplate this for a bit.* CARTER *yawns and turns back to his friend.*)

CARTER: Seriously...can I see her?

TOM: No.

CARTER: Tom, that's not very...I said some stuff and I'm sorry. I didn't know you two were dating.

TOM: It's ...I just took her out a few...she's nice. O K?

CARTER: It's fine. (*Beat*) So, lemme see.

TOM: Jesus... (*Pulls a snapshot out of his wallet*) I'm holding it.

CARTER: That's mature. (*Goes over to look at it*) Oh, cool. It's one of those "makeover deals" isn't it?

TOM: I guess. Yes.

CARTER: Very nice. I like the boa.

TOM: Don't be a prick.

CARTER: Kidding! She's sweet. I mean, from meeting her and everything, I could tell.

TOM: Thanks.

CARTER: Does she...I mean, does her weight go up and down or...? I only ask because she's got a nice face, so I'm curious.

TOM: She's not worried about that kind of thing—buy into all of those diet fads...which is sort of refreshing, actually.

CARTER: Sure. I'm just saying...can't turn on C N N without some doctor talking about...

TOM: Because, you know...yeah, I think she's pretty as well, but we don't ever talk about that. "What if?" kinds of shit about her size. She's happy with who she is, and so...it's...

CARTER: Then great. *(Looks again)* Can you please let me...I'm not six years old. I promise not to take it.

TOM: 'kay.

(TOM very warily lets go of the photo. In stages. Finally it is in CARTER's hands. He studies it.)

CARTER: No, I can tell that she's a very genuine person, even from some photo. I like the starburst effect.*(He smiles.)* That's a joke.

TOM: Here, just give it back.

CARTER: Wait...I'm serious, though. Could probably get on one of those reality shows if she lost, like, eighty pounds, she'd be kinda stunning.

TOM: I know, but I just said...here.

CARTER: I mean, I'm only talking. I'm not an expert. Perhaps we should see what everybody in the cafeteria thinks...

TOM: Carter! CARTER, YOU FUCKER!!

(But TOM Is trapped behind his desk and CARTER is off like a rocket—out the door and down the hall. TOM starts to follow but gives up after a second. returns to his desk.)

TOM: ...Bastard. Ahh, screw it. I don't care. I'm not gonna be...whatever.

(A little bell goes off. ding! Tom looks at his computer and sees an e-mail has arrived. He clicks it and reads.)

Tom: "DEAR TOM, FUK U AND UR FAT BITCH. ASSHOLE. LOL." *(Beat)* That's charming...

(Tom starts to type a response but it slowly dissolves as he begins to pound harder and harder on the keys. Finally he stops, exhausted. Pushes it away. Sits)

"Some old territory for the new couple"

(A bedroom. Helen and Tom are lying on top of the covers, watching a movie—she is concentrating, he is kissing her.)

Tom: ....Mmmmmmm. God, you're so....

(Tom continues to kiss Helen as she watches the T V.)

Helen: Tom...hold on...look...

Tom: ...I am. At you...

Helen: Remember this part? *(Pointing)* I think he's just about to...they're gonna find the gold...

(Sound of gunfire, shouts. Helen laughs. Tom looks at her.)

Tom: ...Pretty funny. He got shot.

Helen: Yeah, but it's meant to be...you know. It's a comedy. Mostly.

Tom: Uh-huh. *(Kisses her)* Mmmmmm...

Helen: ...Wait...

Tom: I don't wanna wait...I wanna...well, lots of things. Kiss you. And...more kisses, and...

Helen: But...this is due back tomorrow.

Tom: Oh, O K... *(Laughs)* Here...

Helen: Ummm, don't start with the good stuff...

Tom: You love the good stuff...

HELEN: Yes, but we can't always...ohh, yes, you can keep doing that, actually...

TOM: See?

HELEN: But we should...Tom...

TOM: Can't help it...I love your mouth. Each lip. Both.

HELEN: Thank you. *(Kissing him)* Thanks.

TOM: I really do like the way you kiss. So much.

HELEN: Me too. We fit, you know? Our mouths together. It's important.

TOM: I, yeah...agree...

(HELEN *and* TOM *begin to make out—the movie is forgotten. He reaches around, finds the remote and the sound drops out. After a moment, she gently pulls back, studies him.*)

HELEN: ...So, you feel comfortable with me? I mean...

TOM: I'm...yes. I am. I have honestly never been more relaxed around a person. *(Beat)* Well, my mother, but that gets into a weird area...

HELEN: Ha-ha-ha.

(Beat)

TOM: Seriously, I haven't felt this way for a long time. Ever, probably.

HELEN: I'm glad.

TOM: No, I mean it. *(Kisses her)* I adore you.

HELEN: Me, too. *(She kisses him)* And I wasn't trying to get that out of you...

(HELEN *punches* TOM *playfully on the shoulder, which leads to horseplay. After a moment, he lays ["lies"...] back. relaxed.*)

TOM: God, this feels so damn good! You know? I mean...just laying around here, us together. All alone.

HELEN: I know.

TOM: It's like...I feel like we're on a raft or something. Paddling along, all the time in the world...no one around to bug us. *(Mimes paddling)* Ahhh, this is the life!

HELEN: ...Like the beginning of *Heaven Knows, Mr. Allison.* Remember?

TOM: Exactly! Yep... *(Smiles)* And you could play the Deborah Kerr part. You'd make a very saucy nun...

(HELEN *kisses* TOM *and he slips back into a comfortable position.)*

HELEN: ...Sounds good. *(Beat)* Sorta.

TOM: What?

HELEN: I dunno, I just...I sense something. A kind of being...isolated. At times.

TOM: Helen...haven't I been with you every day? I mean, my friends have even said things. Noticed it. I'm hardly with them any more.

HELEN: But...that's what I mean.

TOM: What?

HELEN: Neither am I. You know? I mean, we've been going out for...how-ever long, and I only met that one guy. Carter. At the restaurant.

TOM: That's true, but...I mean, I've been waiting for the, maybe, a right time or something. One of those office parties or...

HELEN: Tom.

TOM: No, truthfully! I thought maybe on the Fourth or...we do a big party at the beach. A cookout and stuff.

HELEN: Great...should I go with a thong or be a little more conventional?

TOM: Very funny. I was being serious…

(A sort of silence drops over HELEN *and* TOM. *Both of them staring off. Quiet)*

HELEN: …It's just a little like we're, I dunno, hiding or whatever. From people.

TOM: …No…

HELEN: You don't think?

TOM: No, Helen, I really don't. At all. *(Beat)* I mean, we're not exactly hanging out with all your pals, either. We've barely…

HELEN: That's not true—I ask you all the time if you'd want to, or if we…

TOM: …Yeah, but…

HELEN: I'm dying to show you off, Tom, if you'd let me…I've told you to pick me up at work, all kinds of things!

TOM: I know, but…it's a library. Not supposed to talk in there…I'll be in trouble.

HELEN: Tom…please. *(She waits.)* Listen, I had a thing come up for me at the…this opportunity. Remember the interview that I…yeah. That. It's only a couple towns over, but far enough away that…whatever. The point is, it's a great offer and the more I think about this—every time we end up ordering in or you run out to get videos—some little thing in my head, this warning buzzer says, "Watch it. Just watch out".

TOM: Helen…

HELEN: I just hope you're not embarrassed by me in some way, because, well, I mean…I don't know what…

TOM: No. Why would you say that? I'm not at all… what're you…?

HELEN: Nothing. I'm not saying anything, except I need you to be honest with me here. Today, if possible.

TOM: ...well, what am I supposed to say now? To that?

HELEN: Just the truth.

TOM: I'm...I meant something easier.

(HELEN *smiles at this as* TOM *scoots closer to her on the bed, holds her. A kiss*)

TOM: Helen...you can't leave town, I need you around. You're like the sunrise to me. Like Vitamin C or something. My oxygen. *(Beat)* I need you...

HELEN: I'm not looking for fairy tale or out of the ballpark or anything...just a person who cares about me like I do them. Simple.

TOM: ...Love isn't simple. It's...never having to say you're sorry.

(TOM *starts to say more, but* HELEN *stops him. Smiles.*)

HELEN: ...I don't need you to be clever here! No jokes. Or film quotes... Just be very clear...and honest.

(TOM *kisses* HELEN, *then sits her down on the bed. Joins her. Tries to get serious*)

TOM: Fine. Look...I wanna be truthful now, so just let me...you know, bumble along. Alright?

HELEN: Please. Bumble on.

(HELEN *Smiles and* TOM *Slowly returns it to her. He touches her face. Strokes her hair*)

TOM: Helen...I want you. Both mentally and physically. Each curve, every last inch of you... *(He kisses her.)* I'd hope you can see that by now...

(HELEN *starts to speak but* TOM *holds up a finger to silence her.*)

TOM: ...so...I don't know how to do this. To say exactly
how I'm feeling because, you know, I'm a guy and
we're taught how to kick stuff, and tear the wings off
shit—but, look...I can see that we've got something
here, I'm not stupid, right? —do not answer that—
and I need you to know. That I know. I'm really just
so damn...overcome by this. Here. Us. I don't take it
lightly or in some carefree manner at all. No. Helen,
you are just, well, very important to me...very... *(Beat)*
Look, I've fallen for you, fallen hard, and...yeah, I love
you and I hope...

HELEN: Sorry, what?

TOM: I love you.

HELEN: What? I didn't ...

TOM: I love you.

HELEN: Wow.

TOM: So I hope that you give me a chance to prove it
in the near future, at the, afore-mentioned volley-ball-
slash-beach party or at some other to-be-determined
public gathering. And if you take that other job, even
a few towns over, it would be a real, you know. Bad
thing. *(Grins)* O K, that sort've sucked, but most the
ingredients were in there...

HELEN: Yeah...and it was kind of lovely.

TOM: Then, good. Thanks.

HELEN: No, thank you...Tom Sullivan.

TOM: You're welcome...Helen...what's your last name
again?

(HELEN *smacks* TOM *playfully on the shoulder again.*
Twice)

TOM: I know it has, like, a "B" in it.

HELEN: "Bond." *(Laughs)* You ass...

TOM: Right, "Bond", sorry. "Bond."

TOM: Mmmm! *(Kisses her)* You're awesome.

HELEN: You, too, Tom. You're a good man. *(Kisses him back)* Good and strong and brave and…ummmm…lots of nice things…

TOM: …Mmmmmm! I love it when you talk dirty.

(TOM begins to kiss HELEN. More and more. She responds and, after a moment, lets him unfastens her bra. He starts to caress and kiss her there. Her eyes slowly close.)

(Her hand searches around, finds the remote again. Click! Up come the sounds of war and mayhem on the soundtrack. Loud)

"Twists and turns at the office"

(TOM at his desk again. Working. JEANNIE standing nearby with a file in her hand. Waiting)

JEANNIE: …So are you bringing her to the thing next month?

TOM: Huh? *(Looks up)* Oh, yeah. I think.

JEANNIE: Can't decide?

TOM: Ummm, you know…she's gotta check if she can get off from work.

JEANNIE: Oh. I see. And what's she do?

TOM: She's…she's a printed word specialist.

JEANNIE: …ahh. *(To herself)* Perfect.

TOM: What's that?

JEANNIE: Nothing. *(Points)* Are you almost done there? I need to get those out by five…

TOM: Yeah, hold on.

(TOM *goes back to work while* JEANNIE *glances around.
Takes in the space)*

JEANNIE: No pictures of her up yet.

TOM: Nah.

JEANNIE: How come?

(TOM, *frustrated, drops his pen and looks straight at*
JEANNIE.)

TOM: …Wasn't the one that appeared on everybody's
desktop this morning enough? *(Turns his monitor
around)* You need more laughs than this?

JEANNIE: I wouldn't mind.

TOM: Great.

JEANNIE: Yeah, I'd be up for that.

TOM: Jesus…you really are awful, you know that? I
mean it.

JEANNIE: Just keep signing, O K? Your little sermon
isn't needed.

TOM: I'm not…whatever.

JEANNIE: That's exactly right. Whatever.

TOM: …Jeannie…can't we just be…?

JEANNIE: Don't bother. Sign.

(TOM *is about to follow instructions but pulls the files from
his desk and slips them in a drawer. Shuts it. Sits back as he
checks his watch.)*

TOM: No, uh-uh, you've got time. And I want you to
tell me…go on. What the hell I did to you that was so
bad. Do it.

JEANNIE: Tom, don't be a prick, alright? I need to make
FedEx.

TOM: You will…

JEANNIE: No! I'm not obligated to talk with you about shit...we're co-workers, we work together now and that is all. Give me the files.

TOM: Nope.

JEANNIE: You're an asshole...

TOM: Maybe so. I dunno...maybe I am. Or have been to you. That's what I'm saying! If I have, then tell me. Show me how...

(It's a stand-off for a moment, then JEANNIE *makes a move toward* TOM. *He stands up and holds his ground. She backs off and stands to one side, hands on her hips.)*

JEANNIE: ...I don't even wanna discuss your fat bitch, O K? She's...

TOM: Stop that.

JEANNIE: So, forget it. I'll just say about us, I mean, what we've...

TOM: ...No, let's do the whole...

JEANNIE: Fuck you! Don't tell me what we'll do. At all.

TOM: I'm not. I'm just saying we should probably, you know...

JEANNIE: We should've probably done a lot of things! We should probably be engaged now, if you weren't such a spineless shit, like every other guy...so...

TOM: Your mouth is, like, I dunno. Wow.

JEANNIE: Yeah, exactly right. "Wow." I'm twenty-eight years old and I just keep hitting the booby prize and you know what? After a while, it really starts to get you down...

TOM: But, I'm not...that's not my...

JEANNIE: What? Problem? I didn't say that. It's no one's problem, me included... it just sucks. That's what I'm saying. *(Beat)* I thought maybe you were different, but

you ended up being the same kind of lame guy that I
perpetually date and it just freaks me out a little. That
maybe you're the only type's out there. These baby
boys who run around in nice clothes but all they really
wanna do is breast feed for the rest of their days…

TOM: …I can't speak for other people, Jeannie, but I…

JEANNIE: I don't care anymore. I don't.

TOM: I'm just saying that…you and I didn't end up
working out, but it doesn't mean…I like you. I did
always like you, but…we're…

JEANNIE: Tom, I know that you think that means
something to me, but it's really just drivel. O K? More
of the same.

TOM: Fine. I'm sorry.

JEANNIE: And that doesn't do shit, either.

(TOM *nods, then sits and pulls out the files. Signs his name
in several more places and then holds them out.* JEANNIE
goes over and grabs them. Hovers)

TOM: Yes?

JEANNIE: Listen, Tom…

TOM: Don't worry about it, Jeannie.

JEANNIE: You just get me so frustrated.

TOM: It really is fine…

JEANNIE: No, I figure that I should just…I mean, who
knows the next time we might see each other, like,
in a non-professional way, and the thing of it is, the
strange part of it is this—I'd take you back right now.
I'm serious. I would, and I'm not sure why…because
you are not really that…great you weren't so nice to
me, Tom. Not at all. You didn't hit me or anything, do
something that the police might contact you about, but
you really hurt me. A lot. By just being…you know.

You. And yet when I'm sitting here, looking at you I still have all these…whatevers toward you. Feelings and all that stuff, so, yeah. It really is a bit weird still. Tender, or…

TOM: …I understand.

JEANNIE: No, you don't! I mean, no offense but how could you? You're you and sitting over there—I'm a whole other person—so, you can't know how it felt for you to do all that crap to me, 'cause if you did know or could feel it then I, I, I just refuse to believe that you'd've done it, because that'd suck. That would actually suck shit if it were the truth, so no—I'm ruling that out as a possibility. I wanna at least pretend that I was going out with a better guy than that, even if it wasn't true—even if he was secretly thinking that I wasn't good enough or, or cute enough or, just, like, whatever…not enough of something—I'm gonna fool myself into buying that other story because it'd be just way too awful to know that the opposite is what was really going on…that we were out there having fun and being all intimate and whatever, but that you were never really gonna give us a shot at this were you?…at being a couple. Us two.

TOM: Jeannie, I'm…I hear you, I do, but maybe we shouldn't get into all this right now. 'Kay?

JEANNIE: …Fine. That's no surprise. *(Beat)* Look, I know you're with her now—this Helen person—and I said I wasn't gonna…but I really do need to know.

TOM: …Yes? What?

JEANNIE: Come on. Tom. *(Points at screen)* What is the story with that one?

TOM: Jeannie…

JEANNIE: I mean, I hope it's some sort of mothering thing or whatever, 'cause if not, it's just so off-the-charts gross that I don't know what to say.

TOM: We should probably stop now.

JEANNIE: I mean, you know what everybody is saying around here, right? I know that you know. And it doesn't even faze you, huh? At all?

TOM: I'm...I don't wanna do this. Here.

JEANNIE: It's not like she's...she's really fat, Tom! A fat sow and you know it. I can tell you're aware by the way you're acting, which is really the puzzling part...

TOM: I-like-her. End of story.

JEANNIE: Yeah, but what the hell? Did you do something bad in some former life that you're making up for? Tell me, because...she's...well, you know what she's like better than the rest of us...I mean... is she a good cook, or...?

TOM: STOP IT! Jeannie, just stop this. I get that you're pissed at me and you needed to blow off some steam so that's why I, I...I allowed you to say stuff, but...

JEANNIE: You didn't "allow" me shit, Tom! I can say whatever I want, any time I want. The whole company is, why should I be any different?

TOM: Then talk if you want to! I-DO-NOT-CARE!!! I enjoy her because she's not you, anything like you... she is not obsessed with looks and money and clothes and useless bullshit like that! OKAY?! *(Beat)* I like who I am when I'm with her, alright, so just...fuck, leave us alone.

JEANNIE: Ohhhh..."us". So it's us now, huh?

TOM: Yeah. It is.

JEANNIE: And, forgive me for saying it, but she seems a little obsessed with some things...like maybe Dorito's.

(TOM *starts to come around his desk now, determined to put an end to this.* JEANNIE *stares him down.*)

TOM: I'm serious here...you need to go.

JEANNIE: I am going, I am, but not because you say so. Because I want to. I want to be as far away from you as I can be...

TOM: Good.

JEANNIE: Yeah, "good". Nice retort.

TOM: Just...

JEANNIE: What an ass. *(Beat)* I'm sure you thought this would hurt me, right? Like, "What's the worst thing I'd be able to do to her?" And this is what you came up with, some self-image killer like this one...Tom ditched me for fucking Momma Cass! Boo-hoo, woe is me! Is that what all this shit is about, getting back at me?!! Huh?!!!

TOM: Jeannie, get out of here! NOW!!

JEANNIE: It doesn't hurt me at all! NOT ONE BIT!! It just makes you look like some creepy fucker and a totally ...AHHHHHH!!! I don't care. I hate you. HATE-YOU. So, so much.

(JEANNIE *storms out of* TOM's *office, leaving the door wide open. He doesn't have the strength to close it; crosses to his couch instead and sits. Rubs his eyes.*)

(*When he opens them, he sees* CARTER *standing at the door.*)

TOM: ...Go away. Seriously.

CARTER: That's not very neighborly.

TOM: Neighbors don't treat neighbors like that. Enemies barely do...

CARTER: Dude, it's a joke. *(Beat)* Think of it as payback for forwarding everybody my email about that one lady at lunch. And I did see the string of her tampon, by the way…when she crossed her legs.

TOM: …I'm not kidding, Carter…

CARTER: I thought Helen looked good blown up like that! Several people I talked to said they're gonna keep it…   .

TOM: Come on, man. Really. Just leave me alone today.

CARTER: Fine.

(*But instead of leaving,* CARTER *goes and drops into* TOM's *chair and starts playing with it. Swinging in circles and raising/lowering the seat mechanism.*)

TOM: If Moses had needed, like, another plague…I would've given him your number.

CARTER: Bad day?

TOM: I'm getting used to 'em.

CARTER: That's why I'm here. To be, like, a calming influence.

TOM: Great. If you're my best chance, then I'm screwed…

CARTER: Nah. All will be fine, my friend. I promise.

TOM: O K. (*Beat*) I don't even need to ask you why you're here…

CARTER: Just chillin'.

TOM: Uh-huh. Figured.

(CARTER *and* TOM *Sit in their respective spots for a bit, staring up at the ceiling. Finally,* TOM *speaks.*)

TOM: …So, lemme ask you something, then.

CARTER: Shoot.

TOM: And honestly now…just an opinion is all, so no big deal.

CARTER: I'm ready.

TOM: What do you actually think of her? Helen, I mean.

CARTER: Ummmmm…

TOM: Not for you, or, like, scoping her out down in Jamaica or that type of thing…just as a person.

CARTER: Oh. Like that.

TOM: Yes.

(CARTER *sits back in the chair, thinking for a moment.*)

CARTER: …You're begging for trouble.

TOM: That's…why do I even ask you?

CARTER: No, and I'll tell you why! I will. I know that I'm not super familiar with her or anything, like, her qualities—of which there may be many…

TOM: …There are…

CARTER: …and that's great. Terrific. But I'm just talking purely as an "Is this a good deal for my pal here?" thing.

TOM: Fine. And?

CARTER: …And you got a long road ahead, that's all. Just being honest.

TOM: Fine.

CARTER: I'm not saying I don't admire you—I do, actually, 'cause I know that I couldn't do it! —But she's gonna end up a weight around your neck. Forgive the pun…

TOM: You're…doing that strictly on a "physical" basis…which is…

CARTER: Of course! Fuck, what else can I go on? *(Beat)* I don't wanna come off like some Elton John here, but you're a good-looking guy. You're successful, bit of a player in the industry…I don't understand you taking God's good gifts and then pissing on 'em…

TOM: Carter…

CARTER: Dude, you're the one who evoked a biblical thing earlier…so take a glance at Noah and all that flood shit! He didn't pair up the apes with the antelope, right? It's one of the many laws of nature. "Run with your own kind."

TOM: That is so…out of whack that I'm, like, completely lost now…

CARTER: …Hey, it's a free country and if this is how you really feel, then you are fucking Gunga Din. "Better man than I am" and all that shit. Just do not be surprised when you turn a few heads down at the mall.

TOM: But why can't we…I mean, shit! I dunno, man, I like her. A lot. She makes me happy, and I really wanna make her happy, too…

CARTER: I'm not saying she can't be happy. That she shouldn't meet somebody, but it oughta be a fat somebody, or a bald one. Whatever. Like her. A somebody that fits her…

TOM: That's crazy…things aren't just based on appearance!

CARTER: …Maybe you should snap on the T V once in a while. *(Beat)* …I'm not talking about what people deserve, I'm saying what they get. You look one way, you have access to all this…look some other way, all you get is that. Sorry, but it's true.

TOM: …Yeah, well, it sucks…

CARTER: It's whatever. Truth. People are not comfortable with difference. Ya know? Fags, retards, cripples. Fat people. Old folks, even. They scare us or something.

TOM: I don't think that's true. I mean, I'm not…no, Carter, I don't buy that. We're all…

CARTER: Come on, be honest! The thing they represent that's so scary is what we could be, how vulnerable we all are. I mean, any of us.

TOM: Old people, though? Come on. We're all gonna age. It's…

CARTER: Not me. I hope I'm a goner before then. The elderly make me sick…

TOM: This is…you're not helping me, Carter! That is the most depressing shit I've ever heard. *(Beat)* Seriously.

(CARTER holds up his hands and shrugs. TOM sits up on the couch, thinking. A bit lost)

CARTER: All I'm saying is this…do what you want. If you like this girl, then don't listen to a goddamn word anybody says. Not one. *(Beat)* However…if you're looking for my opinion, it's this—you've got your whole life to be a positive person, O K? To do some good in the community and be a big-hearted fellow or whatever. Overlook people's flaws and plant saplings and shit. But you're only young once. Handsome and youthful and vibrant. So don't fuck it up, that is all I'm telling you here. Don't take a complete dump on your one moment in the sun… *(Beat)* Not for somebody like her.

TOM: Carter…Fuck! You're not… God…you don't always have to say something. You know? Like, every-thing that comes into your head. I mean…shit.

(TOM catches himself, stops. silence. After a minute, CARTER yawns and slowly stands.)

CARTER: Yeah, I should stuff an envelope or two. *(Laughs)* So look…I wanna run this past you first,

I mean…I'm gonna ask Jeannie to that beach deal coming up. Is that cool?

TOM: Ummm…sure. No, of course.

CARTER: I mean, no weirdness for us?

TOM: None. I think you two could… just might be perfect for each other.

CARTER: Yeah, me too! *(Beat)* I heard she's started going to a gym, so that's something. I mean, you know her body, right? Obvious potential…

TOM: 'Course.

CARTER: Anyway…as long as we're still…

TOM: Sure. I think we'll remain exactly what we are. You and me.

CARTER: Friends, right?

TOM: Sorta. *(Gestures with his fingers)* About this much…

CARTER: Good enough for me. Oh I forgot. *(He reaches into a shirt pocket and hands* TOM *the photo of* HELEN *that he took before. Pats* TOM *on the shoulder)* I know you'll do the right thing.

(CARTER exits. TOM goes to the couch and sits down. Holds the picture in front of him. Brings it closer now. Staring at it. Hard)

"One of those blustery days at the beach"

(A stretch of sand. TOM, *in a flowered swimsuit, sitting alone on a blanket. Trying to focus on a biography)*

(After a moment, JEANNIE *approaches. She is looking fit and is wearing a skimpy bikini. She towers over him.)*

JEANNIE: …Thought that was you.

TOM: Yeah. Hey. *(Jumps up)* …You look good. I mean, nice.

JEANNIE: Thanks. Yeah…I'm doing Pilates now. *(Beat)* How come you guys are sitting way down here?

TOM: Oh, we're just…little privacy, I suppose. Edge of the group is all.

JEANNIE: Ah. Cool.

TOM: So… *(Beat)* You and Carter, huh?

JEANNIE: Yeah, how 'bout that?!

TOM: It's good.

JEANNIE: I hope so. He's actually O K once you get him outta the office…

TOM: Most people are. That's not, like, the best environment for a person. Those cubicles…

JEANNIE: Probably not. *(Smiles)* Anyways…

TOM: Right. Anyway. I hope you guys…

JEANNIE: …thanks. You, too, I guess.

(JEANNIE leans toward TOM and he gives her a peck on the cheek.)

JEANNIE: Well…come down and do a little volleyball later or something.

TOM: Will do. Maybe.

JEANNIE: 'Kay. *(Beat)* See that you're still wearing that swimsuit I got you…

TOM: Yes. I like it.

JEANNIE: Looks good on you. I mean, nice. *(Grins)* Alright, so I'll see you, then…

TOM: O K. Take care.

JEANNIE: Same to you. *(Hangs on)* And, look, about all that other stuff…

TOM: Don't worry about it, Jeannie, it really is fine…

JEANNIE: O K, yeah, but I just want you to know that… that I'm…

(HELEN *arrives on the scene juggling a large tray full of food. She is wearing a one-piece suit, with a beach wrap around her waist.*)

JEANNIE: Hey. Get everything you need?

HELEN: Yes, thanks. *(To* JEANNIE*)* Hello.

JEANNIE: Hi, I'm Jeannie. Tom and I…work together.

HELEN: Oh, nice. I'm Helen.

JEANNIE: Yeah, I figured. *(Beat)* …I just mean, Tom mentioned you before.

HELEN: Oh. *(Hugs* TOM*)* That was sweet.

TOM: Hey.

JEANNIE: Anyhow, I came down to say "hello" and invite you guys over for some games later…

TOM: Cool. We'll, ummm…

HELEN: I'm not too sporty, but…not that you could tell or anything!

(HELEN *and* JEANNIE *share a little laugh.* JEANNIE *glances at* TOM, *who tries to smile but only grimaces.*)

TOM: We'll see. Thanks, though.

HELEN: Yes, we appreciate it. And really great to meet you…

JEANNIE: You, too. So long, Tom.

TOM: O K. Bye, Jeannie…

(JEANNIE *throws one last look at* TOM, *then heads off down the beach toward the others. He sits down on the blanket with the food.* HELEN *follows in a moment, out of breath.*)

TOM: …So. That's Jeannie. She's in accounting.

HELEN: …That's quite a swimsuit she's got there. For an accountant. *(Recovers)* Seems nice, though.

TOM: Yeah. Pretty much.

HELEN: What's that mean?

TOM: Oh, ya know…have our differences at work sometimes, that's all.

HELEN: Ahh.

(HELEN and TOM settle themselves on their blanket and begin to sort the food items into two stacks.)

TOM: Oh, good, I'm glad they had those kettle chips…. *(He looks off.)* Is that Carter?

HELEN: Yeah, he said "hi" when I was down there. He introduced me around.

TOM: Good, that's— *(Yells)* HEY, BUDDY! *(Laughs)* Yeah, right! Sure!!

HELEN: You can go down there if you want.

TOM: Huh? No, I wanna be here with you. We'll, you know…later.

HELEN: 'Kay. *(Looking up)* Beautiful day.

TOM: Uh-huh, yep. Super nice…

(HELEN and TOM sit for a moment, taking in the sun. The surf)

HELEN: How long do these things usually go? Any idea?

TOM: Ummm, no, but…we don't have to stay or anything. That's fine. I just need to, you know, make an appearance…

HELEN: No, I like it. Being here with you and all your… it's great. *(Beat)* We just promised those guys that we'd…at some point drop off the cheque…

TOM: Oh, right, the travel agent. Sure. *(Beat)* We should maybe…later. Go.

HELEN: Hmm, weird vibe here. Tom are you sure…?

TOM: …yeah. You kidding me? It's a…great place. I love Miami.

HELEN: I sorta meant about the part where we get to be together, but…

TOM: Oh, that. *(Yawns)* Yeah, that's O K.

(HELEN *swats him on the arm.* TOM *reacts and sits back. She watches him as he turns away.)*

HELEN: So, are you excited about it? The trip I mean?

TOM: What? Of course. *(Beat)* It's all set and everything.

HELEN: That's not really the same as just saying "yes".

TOM: Jesus, fine…yes. Better? *(Beat)* Food looks good. Thanks for going down there…

HELEN: Figured we should grab some before it was gone…

TOM: Right. Sorry, I should've…

HELEN: No, it felt nice, to walk through the surf like that. Fun.

TOM: Cool. Glad you could make it…

HELEN: …it wasn't that far.

TOM: No, I'm…I meant, switch days or whatever.

HELEN: I know. It's a joke. *(Beat)* Tom are you sure?

TOM: Of course. Why?

HELEN: I'm…nothing. Let's eat.

TOM: No, Helen. What?

HELEN: Same ol' stuff. Doesn't matter.

TOM: Of course it does. Of course… Tell me.

HELEN: Look where we're at. I mean, Tom, it's…forget it. *(Holds up a hot dog)* Ketchup?

TOM: This isn't…Helen, I just wanted to get us near the sea wall here, so we'd have a little protection from the wind. That's all.

HELEN: Tom…

TOM: I'm serious!

HELEN: But we haven't…we hardly talked to…

TOM: …I introduced you to people…

HELEN: In the parking lot! As you and I were unloading stuff out of the car. That's not an introduction.

TOM: …Shit. I knew this would happen!

HELEN: You knew it would happen because you know who you are, Tom. I don't think you're ready for this.

TOM: Come on, I don't wanna fight…just eat something, alright?

HELEN: It's not fighting, Tom. When you and I talk, that's not fighting. It's talking. That's what people do.

TOM: Whatever.

HELEN: Tom…what's going on?

TOM: Nothing.

(Long silence between HELEN *and* TOM. *The sound of the ocean)*

HELEN: I told you…I've always said that you needed to be honest. More than anything else.

TOM: I know. I know that…

HELEN: But you're not…this isn't…

TOM: Helen, come on, stop now! Shit…this is my company picnic, O K? We're supposed to be having some fun.

HELEN: "Fun." O K... *(She slowly stands.)* Let's go join in the big game.

(HELEN *jumps up and down a few times, miming a few shots as* TOM *watches. He looks over to where his friends are.)*

HELEN: Come on, Tom! It's fun!!

TOM: Stop it! Stop!! *(Grabs her)* Helen, please stop that.

HELEN: Fine. Then let's chat, ok? *(She sits again.)* Because it's pretty damn hard to sit out here with a fake smile plastered on my face...

TOM: Alright.

(HELEN *and* TOM *sit in silence for a moment, then she reaches over and grabs a piece of chicken. Starts to eat. He sits and watches her—finally he has to say something.)*

TOM: ...Come on, slow down a little bit, honey. Jesus.

HELEN: Sorry. *(Beat)* I can't help it. I eat when I get stressed out...

TOM: It's fine. Me, too. Sorta.

(HELEN *nods at this. Doesn't believe him. She waits.)*

HELEN: Tom...you're aware of how I feel about you. You already know that.

TOM: Yes.

HELEN: But I get the feeling...I mean, it is now pretty obvious, that we're starting to have problems here... Issues, or whatever. And we need to get over them or...well, you know. Things that I don't wanna think about.

TOM: I guess.

(HELEN *waits for* TOM *to say more, but he keeps staring off toward the others. He is about to say something. Stops)*

HELEN: Please, you need to stay in this. Focused on it, so don't drift off or anything. *(Beat)* ...I love you so much, I really do. Tom. Feel a connection with you that I haven't allowed myself to dream of, let alone be a part of, in so long. Maybe ever. But I can't be with you if you're feeling something other than that same thing that I am...completely and utterly open to that other person. I don't know what I should say here. I'm worried sick. Look at me, when did you ever see me not finish eating something that was placed in front of me? Huh? *(She tries to grin.)* I know you hate those jokes, sorry, but I'm...Tom, tell me about it. I know you're thinking something so we might as well just... one more thing. Just this. And I've never offered this to anyone, not any other person in the world. Ever. My family, or a...no one. *(Beat)* I would change for you. I would. I don't mean Slim-Fast or that one diet that the guy on T V did...with the sandwiches from Subway. That guy...

TOM: Helen...that...that's not...

HELEN: ...I'll do something radical to myself if you want me to. Like be stapled or have some surgery or whatever it takes—one of those rings—because I do not want this to end. I'm willing to do that, because of what you mean to me. The kind of, just, ecstasy that you've brought me. So...I just wanted you to know that.

(TOM sits there, taking it all in. Looking off. HELEN nudges him with an elbow.)

HELEN: ...This would be an excellent time to say something sweet to me. If you at all care about my feelings.

TOM: I know. I'm... *(Beat)* Helen, that was such a nice thing to offer.

HELEN: ...Oh-my-God...

TOM: What?

HELEN: I just…the way you worded that right then. In the "past" tense. It scares me.

TOM: No, I just…it is. Really. And I appreciate it so much.

HELEN: …But what? *(Beat)* Gosh, I wish those thousand ships would show up right about now…

TOM: Yeah… *(Long beat)* Helen, look, I've been thinking…

HELEN: …O K.

TOM: I think you are an amazing woman, I honestly do. And I really love what we have here. Our moments together…but I think that maybe, you know, some time would be good here, or if you were to, I'm not sure….maybe take that job. It might tell us if we're… I dunno.

HELEN: Oh… *(Beat)* Wow, that's a bit of a….you know…I mean, it's…

(HELEN *tries to interrupt again but* TOM *stops her. Waits)*

TOM: Listen…if we were in some other time or a land that nobody else was around on…like that island from the movie, the Sinatra film—*None But the Brave*—then everything might be O K, I wouldn't be so fucking paranoid about what the people around me were saying. Or even thinking. Then it could just be you and me and that'd be so great. Perfect. But…I guess I do care what my peers feel about me. Or how they view my choices and, yes, maybe that makes me not very deep or petty or some other word, hell, I dunno! It's my Achilles flaw or something. I'm…

(TOM *stops for a moment, regrouping.* HELEN *tries to speak.)*

HELEN: …Tom, don't do this, O K? Please don't. We can, I dunno…we…

TOM: No, I need to…if I stop now I'm not gonna be able to…finish, so I'm… *(Beat)* Helen…things are so tricky, life is. I know now I'm not really deserving of you, of all you have to offer me. I can see that now. I want to be better, to do good and better things and to make a proper sort of decision here, but I…I can't. I cannot do it. I mean, I could barely drive here today because of…my hands were shaking the whole time. They were. Jumping up and down on the wheel there. And these are all people that I know! That I…I'm just not gonna be able to do this, on, like, a daily basis. *(Starts to cry)* God…look at me! It's…I'm sorry about this and I wish that I was saying what you wanna hear. I do. That would make me really happy, to please another person right now. I mean, a person that I'm feeling this…love for. Yeah, love. But sometimes it just isn't enough. You know? All this love inside and it's not nearly enough to get around the shit that people heave at you…I feel like I'm drowning in it—shit—and I don't think I can…I don't wanna fight it any more. I am just not strong enough for that, so I'm gonna lay on my back for a while and float. See if I can keep my head above the surface. *(Beat)* I guess that's what I needed to say to you. That I'm not brave. I'm not. I know you want me to be…always believed that I can be, but I'm a weak and fearful person, Helen, and I'm not gonna get any better. Not any time soon, at least…

(HELEN *and* TOM *sit quietly, not touching. He is still tearful.)*

HELEN: …But that's…it's something we could work on, right…can't we, Tom? Right?

TOM: …No. I don't think I can.

(HELEN slowly turns away. TOM continues to cry. Big rolling tears with his face turned straight out.)

(They sit together, quiet. Both staring out to sea)

(Silence. Darkness)

END OF PLAY

CPSIA information can be obtained
at www.ICGtesting.com
Printed in the USA
LVHW020346140820
663095LV00014B/1730